J.D. NETTO

YOU ARE NOT *for* EVERYBODY

an honest conversation about branding, storytelling, and audience building

You Are Not For Everybody: An Honest Conversation About Branding, Storytelling, and Audience Building
© Copyright 2024 by J.D. Netto

Cover design © 2024 by J.D. Netto Designs
Interior by J.D. Netto Designs
ISBN: 979-8218484125

Dedicated to my husband.
No, love. We aren't for everyone.
And we know it.

ACKNOWLEDGEMENTS

Though writing a book can be a very lonely journey, one cannot finish the race without love and support. I, for one, couldn't have gotten here without my family, friends, and clients.

If you've ever worked with me on a branding, design, or copywriting project, then you're the reason this book exists. Thank you for believing in my work.

To my beautiful family, thank you for always supporting my ideas. You continue to inspire me daily.

To my husband, thank you for inspiring me to grow as a person, entrepreneur, and artist. I am better because of you.

To my dear friend, Mayte Carvalho, your words during a brunch on a very cold morning in New York City inspired this book. Thank you for your friendship.

To my agent, Susan Velazquez, and my entire team at JABberwocky Literary Agency: thank you for being my cheerleaders and for challenging me to see beyond the now. I am forever grateful to you.

Thank you to my readers. You've been with me for over a decade, and this book also exists because your passion for my novels challenged me to become a better wordsmith.

Last but not least: if this is the first time you've heard of me, thank you for taking a chance on this man's words. May they inspire you to live an authentic and bold life.

CONTENTS

FORE**WORD**
MAYTE CARVALHO

MAYTE
CARVALHO

is the best-selling author of *Persuasion - How to Use Rhetoric and Persuasive Communication in Your Personal and Professional Life* and *Dare to Speak Up.* She is a fellow researcher at the Berkeley Global Society's Institute of Technology and Innovation.

She holds a Master's degree in Communication and Semiotics from PUC-SP. Maytê teaches at ESPM, the PUC MBA program, and Casa do Saber. She previously served as Director of Business Strategy at TBWA\Chiat\Day Los Angeles (one of the world's top five advertising agencies) in California and currently holds the position of Chief Growth Officer at Cubo in New York.

She won The Apprentice - Special Edition and participated in The Return edition. Maytê also has experience as an entrepreneur and was named one of the top six female entrepreneurs in Brazil by GQ Magazine for her 'Pharmacy Beauty' app, which reached the #1 spot on the App Store. She secured investment for her startup with Camila Farani on Shark Tank.

On Instagram and YouTube, she shares intelligent and accessible content on Communication, Marketing, and Sales with her over 100,000 followers.

YOU ARE NOT
FOR EVERYBODY

is a message I wish I had known earlier in my life and career. As women, part of our socialization involves being liked and loved—we are often conditioned to believe that love is earned through likability. This means sitting with your legs closed, speaking in a certain tone, avoiding revealing clothes to be taken seriously, and other similar restrictions—sexism, in a nutshell.

As an author and entrepreneur who was in the public eye at the age of 18 due to my participation in The Apprentice in Brazil, I had to deal with haters and fans at a very young age. I learned that when you allow others to dictate who you are, you give them power over your narrative. This is especially difficult when you're young and exposed on national television, which inevitably comes with its own set of traumas.

Being labeled as a "difficult woman to deal with" became part of my brand, even though I saw myself as kind and gentle. I learned that you have no control over how others perceive you, who they decide you are, or what your words mean to them.

Meaning is a crucial construct when we talk about branding. I've worked for over 15 years in large advertising agencies such as TBWA\Chiat\Day Los Angeles, Grey, and Accenture for clients like Pepsico and Unilever. In every branding decision—whether it was creating a tagline, a key visual, or a brand positioning POV—the critical question was always: What is the meaning behind this logo, this message, or this choice of celebrity? Who is our target audience, and what does it mean to them?

Audience is everything, and meaning changes depending on the audience. For instance, if you were raised in a military household and attended military school, the word "order" might evoke familiarity and peace. However, if you are the fifth child of a hippie couple raised in a Waldorf school, "order" might mean something entirely different. It's the same word but different meanings.

If I ask you now to close your eyes and think about a blue balloon, some of you might picture a hot air balloon—like the ones in Cappadocia— while others might think of a birthday party balloon. Both are balloons, both are blue, but the meanings are different. Communication is an expectation, and you can't always guarantee that others will understand you exactly as you intend. But that's the beauty of it. Your message is not for everybody.

The courage to be your authentic self, even if it means being disliked by some, is a crucial understanding, not only in terms of personal branding but also in self-knowledge as a whole. It's what years of psychoanalysis have taught me, and I'm still learning to make peace with it. That's why this book is not just about branding per se; it's about self-awareness and consciousness.

JD Netto's book feels like a chat with a good friend at a café. It's like scrolling through someone's stories, absorbing million-dollar advice in a casual and genuine way. His personal stories and ethos, intertwined with valuable takeaways, are worth a thousand MBAs. If you are an entrepreneur, creative, or curious person, this book is a must-read.

I am proud to call him a personal friend and to have access to all his wisdom on a personal level. I am also thrilled that the world now has access to his stellar advice.

J.D.
NETTO

INTRODUCTION

You and I are at a coffee shop. There's a fire burning to keep the chill outside as we order our drinks. The bit of chatter going on is not so loud that we can't hear each other, but just enough to feel the possibilities around us. This is what I want you to imagine as you read this book.

You are not holding a guide or textbook. And I'm not a teacher standing in front of a whiteboard. This is a conversation. A very honest one—a collection of experiences, research, and lessons learned in the field of branding, marketing, and narrative. It's meant to spark thoughts, ideas, and the reflection of self.

Allow me to get candid. College wasn't for me. It's not that I didn't want to attend, but life kicked me out of the nest before I knew how to use my wings.

This conversation is based on seventeen years of experience as an entrepreneur of the arts. While I am a jack of many trades, some truths are irrefutable. These are the truths comprising this book, regardless of your current field of expertise (or the one you dream of exploring).

Out of all the irrefutable truths in the world, there's one that will lift a heavy weight off your shoulders. Not everyone will be fond of who you are or the message you carry. And that's a good thing.

Before we talk business, I need to introduce you to rejection. I get it. You're probably wondering, *J.D., are we already going there? I haven't even sipped my coffee yet, and you're coming for me. I thought this was about brand building and marketing? What's with the deep talk?* Buckle up! Because to explore those topics, we must take a deep dive into ourselves first.

In my early twenties, I queried various agents hoping my first fantasy novel would get representation. I can't tell you how passionate I got writing those emails. In my mind, passion was enough to get them to reply with a request for the full manuscript.

All I received was a slew of rejection letters with a message clear as day: There's no audience for this book. But I had written it, and I sure as hell would've read it if I'd found it at a bookstore. Those writing the emails weren't fond of the story because they weren't the target audience. Their rejection didn't mean there was no audience to explore. I knew many shared the same interests as me.

I became somewhat of a recluse after those letters. Call it ego, drive, whatever you want to name it. I locked myself away to read books on writing and watch tutorials about running successful campaigns. I designed my own book cover after analyzing every cover in my genre to see what connected with readers, and I hired an editor to polish the manuscript.

Releasing that first fantasy novel was my college experience—a very public one. The book sold thousands of copies. It gave me a readership and led me to work with incredible people. I can't lie and say that everything was smooth sailing. I got a lot of things right, but I also failed at many of them.

The willingness to prove other people wrong wasn't the driving force behind my will to get the book out. It was rejection that made me take the first step toward the unknown. It was rejection that inspired me to find the hidden path of opportunity. I did it so I could make tangible what I already knew in my heart. That yes, I'm not for everybody. But I am still for somebody.

Countless people never bring their projects to life because they fear rejection. They are paralyzed, wasting energy on the "what ifs" instead of exploring the "what nows." Let's get something out of the way. Rejection is part of the game, but you can turn it into an asset rather than a liability.

Human nature is about connection. We're designed for it. But often, in our desire to connect, we forget that with likes comes dislikes. That's just the way things go. A lot is said about building a loyal audience. Not much is said about the ocean of disagreement that follows.

By the end of this conversation, you'll learn to embrace rejection and use it for your benefit. You will be inspired to craft a narrative so powerful, those who are for you will find you, and those who aren't will not stop talking about you.

A LOT IS SAID ABOUT
BUILDING A LOYAL AUDIENCE.
NOT MUCH IS SAID ABOUT
THE OCEAN OF DISAGREEMENT
THAT FOLLOWS.

WHO ARE YOU?

You can't build a brand without exploring who you are. And like the human mind, a brand evolves with time. The "you" of ten years ago is vastly different from the "you" of today. You may have the same values, relationships, and possess facets that have largely remained the same, but a lot in you has changed.

A brand consists of pillars inspired by the mind of its maker. The moment an individual decides to build their brand, they make a conscious decision to look inward. To make it simple, your brand is rooted in your purpose, no matter the industry or talent.

Someone who's secure in their identity has already built a strong foundation for a brand. Knowing what you like, stand for, and aim to do will inspire you to not only embrace your ideas, but build a platform to share them.

Some reality TV celebrities are fully aware of the influence that comes with a strong identity (and the process of discovering that identity). While some claim they don't deserve their spotlight or influence due to their lack of talent, they are holding people's attention by simply being who they are—no matter how questionable their decisions may be.

These shows keep gripping audiences because their narratives are crafted around the good, the bad, and the ugly. As you might've seen before, these shows and their protagonists aren't afraid to embrace their truth (or their lies, however you choose to see it).

Let's look at this from a storytelling angle. Every story starts by introducing the main character, their world, and the conflict. In most stories, it is through the conflict and discovery of self that they find love.

Experiencing a brand for the first time is a lot like going on a first date. Yes, we're going there. Do let me know if you need time to get back in line for some cake or a pastry. No? Gotcha!

Imagine you match with someone on an app. After exchanging numbers, you text for a while and agree to meet in person. There was a spark—something that told you seeing them would be worth your time. You're on your way to the date and keep thinking about that funny thing they said and the picture that made you blush, when you see them. And they see you. You're a bit guarded at first. Do they look like their photos? Are they as eloquent in person as in their texts? Will the spark stay lit?

You sit at the table, and the conversation begins. You're analyzing their behavior, beliefs, and mannerisms. There's a rush of emotion running through you. If the date goes well, more texts and dates will hopefully culminate in a relationship. If not, then that's it. The boat sank before it sailed.

First dates are about impressions. There's no denying it. Both parties are calculating every move to see if the other will be worth the effort. But more than observing outward traits, we are longing for the spark—that intangible feeling.

That's where dating and branding share a lot in common. Your potential audience will constantly go on first dates with your brand, and it must be as good in person as it is on paper. Every detail matters. It's about how you look at the other person and your tone of voice. It's the topic of conversation, the way you draw them in, and the way they engage with you. It's the little details and mannerisms that keep you both excited.

Look at James Cameron's hit movie *Titanic*. I'm going to go ahead and assume that if you're holding this book, you're old enough to have seen this '97 classic. But I understand we have an entire generation who hasn't watched it, so please, do so if you haven't become a fan like me. You won't regret it.

Put aside the historical event and step past the tragedy of it all, what you get is the story of a young woman who has one unforgettable first date on the poop deck of the grandest ship in the world with a random man from steerage. In the rush of emotions, she found herself wanting more.

Jack pays attention to what Rose needs. She has money but is trapped by societal standards. She isn't what others expect and is fighting to break free. She craves uncharted waters (pun intended). And he can give her that, even without a dime in his pocket. They each have what the other needs. Jack's brand is adventure, while Rose's is freedom. Say what you want about the speed in which they fall in love, but the story works.

The point is that we're all in the business of feeling. It's the human heart that creates connection, not a mere product or entity. You can build a brand around a product, but you can also have a personal brand that will exist beyond anything you do or don't release.

In the end, whatever path you choose, people will seek out the spark over anything else. It's all about how you make them feel.

Why do you think companies invest so much in events that immerse people in their brand, therefore discovering their products? Look at expos. You head to a convention center to network and discover new brands by means of immediate experiences.

Movie premieres, pre-screenings, red carpet events. These are all first impressions that inspire you to feel a certain way toward the brand and product.

We are *all* in the business of feeling.

Coffee shops do not only sell coffee. They sell a creative environment where you can enjoy good food and get some work done. Disney does not sell theme parks. They sell dreams and the chance to be a child again. Luxury brands sell status—they are a symbol you work hard to be who you are.

In the same way feelings guide us, the intangible part of your brand will steer your audience closer or farther from you. There's no way around it.

The simple truth is you cannot build a brand without a foundation. And that foundation needs to be rooted in the core of who you are. The colors of your logo, the design of your website, every visual must convey the emotions you expect the audience to feel when consuming your product or service.

Let's do an exercise together. Feel free to use the space below, grab a notebook, or open the notes app on your phone. Write down your passions. And I do mean your *passions*.

Pay attention to how you feel when something comes to mind. Do you get butterflies? Jitters? Does it make you smile? Your passions are a compass. We can only thrive and grow when we are passionate. And in case you're wondering, *But J.D., how do I identify my passions?* Here's my own little trick. Much like when falling in love, passion for your purpose and goals can be identified by how much real estate it takes up in your mind. The word 'passion' has many meanings, but let's stick to the one I found on Merriam-Webster: a strong liking or desire for or devotion to some activity, object, or concept.

Alright, back to the exercise. Next to each passion, write down a skill you possess that can turn it into reality. Here's some examples: *I love to cook and can make a mean steak. I love to travel and can edit a 30-second video about my experience in an hour. I love public speaking and am very eloquent in front of the mirror.*

It feels good to be honest with ourselves about what we can do. We're often honest about our mistakes, or the lack thereof. Read what you wrote and pay close attention once again to how you feel.

The first time I expressed my feelings on paper was at the age of four. I don't remember drawing the piece (my parents saved it), but I do remember why I loved the story. The crucifixion of Christ fascinated me. And not for the reasons you might think.

The spectacle and drama drew me in. My aunt had an illustrated Bible in her house I would flip through whenever I visited. Despite the many stories, it was the picture of the crucified man between two thieves that intrigued me.

Over the years, my fascination with religion led me to discover tales just as grand—big epics such as Michael Crichton's *Jurassic Park* and J.R.R. Tolkien's Middle-earth. I loved how stories, visuals, music—art—had the power to engross the mind and make you forget your surroundings. I started perusing through magazines on science, paleontology, and history. Until one day, I found a fashion magazine at a friend's house. Curious, I picked it up and boom. There was a spread of two men sharing a very passionate kiss. I don't remember what cologne it was advertising, but God, do I remember how the ad made me feel. I think that was the day I knew I was gay.

But more than an ad helping me affirm my sexuality, I was taken by the notion that a cologne was being sold through a gay kiss. This was the mid-nineties in a small town of Brazil. I can't say my surroundings were progressive back then, but even at a young age, I knew I'd remember the ad for years to come. Whether through inspiration or shock, the campaign had done its job.

I noticed the power of narrative not only in books, movies, and music, but in the pieces marketing them: posters, videos, album covers, etc.

During my teenage years, I attended Joseph P. Keefe Technical High School in Framingham, MA. Freshman year was about exploring all twenty-one shops. I failed miserably at being a carpenter, a hairdresser, and a cook, but then visual arts came along.

I excelled in structuring a comic book story with visuals. I created a board game, crafted an entire campaign for a bottle of milk, and designed my first business card. I realized that my passions aligned with my skills.

Years later, I learned that narrative is an essential part of selling a product (art-related or not). I discovered my love for stories and honed my craft. I noticed that, more than pretty visuals, my clients loved when I explained the message behind them. Suddenly, there was a lot more value to what I created.

Writing books. Graphic design. Brand strategy. J.D. Netto Creative. All these endeavors are a culmination of my passion for storytelling.

Go back to our exercise. Read it one more time. So I ask again. Who are you? What is life reflecting back at you? Don't fall in love with the idea of being something. Fall in love with the journey that will get you there. Those experiences will be the heartbeat of your brand.

THE POINT IS THAT WE'RE ALL
IN THE BUSINESS OF FEELING.
IT'S THE HUMAN HEART THAT
CREATES CONNECTION, NOT A
MERE PRODUCT OR ENTITY.

AN AUDIENCE THAT STAYS

No, talent isn't enough to build an audience. There's more to cultivating followers than being good at something. Many people are overshadowed by their talent because they think it immediately qualifies them for relevance. Well, sorry to say, but it doesn't.

You're scrolling through social media and stumble upon a video of a singer. They're singing an original, and you think their voice is pretty, so you click on their account. That's when you see them covering one of your favorite songs. The one someone you loved used to sing when you were young. It's in that moment you are converted from a mere listener to a fan. You click the "follow" button.

Now you want to know this artist's backstory. You research their upbringing, struggles, victories, favorite brands. You're looking for the rags-to-riches story we love from our favorite shows. You want to know where they stand on certain issues, their opinions, likes, and dislikes.

Talent is a bridge people can walk on or walk off. Don't believe me? Think about artists you enjoyed in your teenage years. Some you still love and occasionally listen to. Others make you cringe. Their talent didn't poof into thin air. Your interest in them did because they stopped making you feel a certain way.

Feel what, J.D.? Something. Curiosity. Anguish. Fear. Inspiration. What happens after you watch a documentary inspired by an artist? You go back to their music, books, movies, products, etc. You reminisce, and once again, that artist is on your mind not because of talent, but because of feeling.

Curiosity becomes loyalty when talented people make you *feel*. Artists are, after all, the essential workers of our hearts. We need music to get through breakups, books for an escape, and so on.

Entrepreneurs are artists. They inspire with their boldness to tread new ground. It's an intense job to not only run a business, but find new ways to stay relevant.

But J.D., will I spend my entire life aiming for relevance? Does it ever stop?

Well, think of it this way. You may not talk to your best friend every day, but when you do, it's as if no time at all has passed. The same happens with an audience you've poured your heart and soul into. Even if you disappear for a while, they'll be willing to rediscover the new you.

This is different from turning away from someone you once followed, listened to, read, or bought from. Here's an example, Evanescence is my favorite band. Their album *Fallen* had such a tight grip on me, I started writing poetry because of it.

It took the band three years to release a new record. During that time, I became loyal to new rock bands, products, and movies. But the moment I saw a banner on their website announcing *The Open Door*, I bought the new album immediately.

Audiences follow because they feel. You root for your favorite sports team out of a sense of pride. You follow someone online because their content sparks feelings. You aren't just a fan of the talent. Talent led you to a community where you belong.

As a child, I was never a big fan of shows or cartoons without structure. I'd watch them if they were on, but I craved a continuous storyline. That was when I became a fan of Japanese animation. Yes, they were dramatic, but their bold narratives and character expressions drew me in. My absolute favorite was *Saint Seiya*, the story of a young orphan chosen to be one of the knights of Athena.

I felt out of place during most of my childhood. In the early 90s, people on my side of town didn't expect little boys to be artists. Never mind gay. So finding a show where a boy who doesn't belong becomes a knight had me hooked.

I was the target audience for the show because I longed for an escape from the world I lived in. I wanted a sense of adventure and awe. To this day, if I am somewhere and spot any-thing relating to *Saint Seiya*, I will peruse the shelves and often make a purchase. I am not just a consumer. I am *still* an active audience member because of the emotional connection I have with the product.

NO, TALENT ISN'T ENOUGH
TO BUILD AN AUDIENCE.
THERE'S MORE TO CULTIVATING
FOLLOWERS THAN BEING
GOOD AT SOMETHING.

UNDERSTANDING NARRATIVE

This is where the secret lies. For you to have a brand and an audience, it's imperative you understand narrative. No, you don't need to be a writer to wield this weapon. You just need to be both aware of the now and one step ahead of it.

Stories are essential for society. We crave them. We love sharing and being a part of them. And we love the communities created by them.

Stories turn us from consumers into audience members. An audience does not exist without a narrative. Whether you're watching your friend's videos online, reading a book, turning on a movie, or sharing some salacious news with a friend, it is narrative that inspires us to take action.

Narrative is a structured story. It introduces an audience to the main players on the board, takes them on an emotional quest, and wraps up the main events with a pretty bow.

Think of your favorite show. The visuals may be stunning,

the acting superb, but if the narrative is predictable, the movie goes from epic to, well, corny. I am not saying predictability is bad. I'm saying it needs to be done with intent.

A narrative makes promises. We want certain characters to win and some to suffer a great demise. But there's one common thread connecting all sorts of narratives. You may like dragons, orcs, and elves, but it is the human experiences that keep us engrossed. It's the tragic death of someone we rooted for and the vengeance taken against the queen we loathe so much. It's the villain winning every battle only to lose the big war.

What happens when your favorite show nears the end? Maybe for the finale, you call your friends and get the snacks. You're ready to feel something. As the episode unravels, you are in awe at how terrible your favorite character's fate is. The credits roll, and lo and behold, the ending didn't live up to your expectations. You talk about it with your friends, on socials, and on forums.

Narrative is what keeps you hooked until the end.

If narrative didn't matter in branding, we'd simply have ad campaigns that said the following:

I am the best shampoo you will ever use.

Toothpaste. Because cavities are a bitch.

Unprotected sex might give you diseases. Use condoms.

I think you get the idea.

Instead, we have writers (hello!) creating an emotional connection between audiences, products, and brands.

Imagine this scenario, you saw an ad for a certain article of clothing. The pictures looked stunning, the video was well edited, and the copy promised you'd feel gorgeous while wearing it. When the box is finally dropped off on your porch, you open it and find the material is of poor quality. You put it on and realize the cut is unflattering. It's nothing like the picture. You look for the return information, only to see the sentence that sends you to customer hell and back: credit only.

Narrative, narrative, narrative. The narrative made you a promise. The narrative led you to believe, and the narrative failed to deliver. Whether for good or ill, you felt something and took action.

Let me give another example you encountered right here in this coffee shop. When you bought your drink at the counter, did you see those three little buttons on the machine with tip percentages? Did you notice that beneath each number was a very specific word: 15% average, 20% good, 25% excellent.

What did you feel as you read each word? Did you immediately give a little something so you didn't come across a certain way? Did you brush it off because, hey, I simply bought some coffee, and I am not obligated to tip someone because they tapped on a screen. Maybe you were compelled to give twenty-five percent because you can. You don't want to be rude. You will forget about the money five minutes later.

See the impact of those three little words? Each one summarized how you might have felt about the service (all positive). This isn't about you being a good or bad tipper. This isn't a discussion of whether or not you should tip. This is about the narrative on that little screen. Suddenly, it's up to you and your conscience to either agree or disagree with the narrative of a positive experience.

I'm sure you've seen those sad commercials about puppies in need of adoption. Trust me, if I could, I'd buy a farm and adopt as many as possible. But I invite you to look at the structure of the commercial.

The music immediately sets the tone for what's to come. Paired with the images of those huge eyes and longing stares is a voiceover that pulls you in. It hits you so hard, you throw out any thoughts of the production value and simply feel the emotions. The narrative has engrossed you to the point that you think of those puppies every time you hear that song.

This happens in every facet of culture: media, shows, books, technology, politics, and more. A perfect example of the power of narrative is religion, and how it grows through stories and testimonies. These narratives are crafted to stir behavior. Do this for a reward. Don't do that, and you'll avoid damnation.

Your favorite TV series creates a cult following because the characters are so three-dimensional, you keep thinking about them after you turn off your device. You talk to your friends about them and dissect every word and action.

Book hangovers are a thing (and I hope this book gives you one) because you are so immersed in the story, you lose track of the time and page count. You simply care about your favorite characters getting the rewards they deserve. Narrative connects you. Narrative drives you, inspires you, and disappoints you.

Apply it to tech. The latest device is coming out, and the entire marketing campaign promised an immersive experience. You want to be surprised as you discover its new features. You want a certain amount of safe unpredictability. But you do want one thing to be predictable—your satisfaction.

In politics, you follow your candidate's campaign. You watch their ads and news outlet appearances, donate, listen to their speeches, and hold on to the promises they make. You vote for who connects with you and your values. It is narrative that differentiates political parties from one another and inspires voters to act.

Narrative is a brand's heartbeat. It's the stories we write and the characters we create that foster community. Let's bring it back to you. How do you apply the concept of narrative to your brand?

Let me share how I structure my novels to connect with readers. I like to write them in four acts. Each act helps me pace the story, understand the motives of every character, and reward the readers who choose to pick up my books.

Act One: The first act serves as setup for the story and world. This is where I introduce readers to the character's motives, struggles, and strengths. This usually consists of an ordinary situation that possess a hint of intrigue. But the ordinary can only last for so long. It must end with an inciting incident—a turning point that will change the character's life forever.

Act Two: This is where the conflict begins—the moment the character's world is shaken up and they must make decisions (clever or foolish). This act must take the story to a midpoint so epic, the character will have no choice but to embrace the struggle and aim for victory.

Act Three: This act exists because the character won't accomplish what they need to do at first. They will fail more than once. This is the moment when the reader can't see how the story will end on a good note. The heroes are tired, the antagonists are winning, and there seems to be no way out.

Act Four: This is the crowning jewel—the moment the reader has been waiting for. The heroes have seen the light at the end of the tunnel and discovered the loophole that will lead them to victory. I reward my readers with the element of surprise. This is the act where I connect all the dots and create an air of mystery around the things I want to keep secret. But in the end, I deliver what I promised the reader.

Allow me to break this down in a way you can apply to your brand:

Act One: Your setup should include an ordinary fact about your audience—something they want (or will want) to change. This is your chance to connect with them where they are. If there's already demand for your product, then this is where your inciting incident will inform them of such demand. If not, this is your chance to create an inciting incident that will produce the demand.

Act Two: Your audience will be thinking about the events of the first act. *How will this product benefit me? How will this person help me? What am I getting out of it?* While your audience ruminates, you act. Stay connected to your audience, but offer them pieces of information that will spur them into action.

Act Three: This act belongs to your audience. If you were clever with your first two acts, your audience will see how they've been failing and will continue to fail if they do not acquire your product. Example: You feel left out if you're not listening to the music everyone's been talking about. Embracing that singer means you are now part of the crew.

Act Four: Your audience is the hero and they have won. What did they win? A crown. And what is the crown? Your product. Now your job is to deliver. You promised a good product? Then it better be good. Because otherwise, this is where a heroic audience turns villainous.

I am happy you've gotten this far. Not so happy that from now on, whenever you watch a movie or read a book, you'll be able pick up on and critique this technique.

THE POINT IS THAT WE'RE ALL
IN THE BUSINESS OF FEELING.
IT'S THE HUMAN HEART THAT
CREATES CONNECTION, NOT A
MERE PRODUCT OR ENTITY.

UNDERSTANDING MARKETING

You're planning a trip with your partner. You want a romantic getaway. You've spent hours online doing research and concluded that Brazil (wink, wink) feels like the adventure of a lifetime. You looked through pictures, researched resorts, and scouted restaurants. You can't stop imagining what it'll be like to explore the dunes in the northeast of the country. But dreaming and planning isn't enough—you have to hop on a plane to make your way to South America.

If branding is the feeling you get when planning a trip, then marketing is the plane ride you take—the vehicle that helps you finally achieve what you desire. And turbulence is always part of the package.

I don't know about you, but I have some wild turbulence stories. Watching videos on social media of people flying out of their seats can be intriguing, but they also fuel my creative brain to think of countless scenarios when I fly. Sometimes we're lucky and have a smooth flight all the way to our destination, but most of the time, there's some shaking along the way. We don't know the pilot, but we trust that those steering the aircraft can make the necessary decisions for a smoother ride.

That's marketing. It's the combination of efforts that lead your audience to your product. Campaigns, ads, commercials, media buying—they all fall under this category. Most of these efforts can be adjusted almost immediately if the campaign hits rough air, and those in charge must act like the pilots, steering toward smoother skies.

This is one of the constant challenges I face when working with creative entrepreneurs. We are often wired to think marketing and branding are the same thing, but they're two different beasts living in the same environment.

Now, let's shift from planes to a store. Imagine you're in the shampoo aisle. As you look through the options, think of the last shampoo commercial you watched. Even if it wasn't recent, it's hard to forget those perfect locks waving in your face, or the actress's look of disappointment as she glances at her damaged tips. They pose the problem in a way that suddenly makes you see your own hair as a beach post hurricane.

The solution comes after the problem is exposed. Everything about the shampoo suddenly screams solution—the logo, colors, visuals, and even the slow-motion shot of the bottle falling into a mysterious white liquid (which I'll assume is milk).

Let me use myself as an example. Whenever I'm about to launch a new book, I always think about the emotional value of my stories. *The Echoes of Fallen Stars* series was written for queer readers who never thought they could be the heroes of a story; Henderbell is an ode to a time when we all believed in magic; *Winterborne* is for the misfit who's always wanted to belong; *The Other Side of the Ocean* was written to shed light on many undocumented issues in America, and *The Broken Miracle* books are for those who believe in the impossible.

While that sounds beautiful on paper, it's my job—and the job of my team—to get these books into the hands of readers looking for the solutions these stories present. That's where marketing comes in: ads, partnerships, out-of-home campaigns, livestreams, etc.

The essence of the product doesn't change, but everything within the marketing sphere can shift in an instant. If an ad is underperforming, you can change the ad, but at that stage, you can't change the product itself.

Marketing determines the perceived value of a product. Look at luxury brands and how they advertise. Have you ever seen a Prada blowout sale? Dior? Nope. And if you have, I'm sorry to say, but you bought a fake one, darling.

Luxury brands focus on exclusivity. Blowout sales target the masses. Luxury marketing efforts never dilute the brand because their monetary value is tied to the exclusivity of owning their product.

While a sale is great for quick cash, it can also imply that those items will quickly depreciate in value. Apple, for example, offers student incentives, but it has never run a blowout sale. Apple sells creativity, and creativity is priceless.

Since branding is emotion and marketing is practicality, let's get practical with a few essential steps for a successful marketing campaign.

AUDIENCE RESEARCH

Do your due diligence and identify your target audience. How much is your audience willing to pay for what you have to offer? Where do they shop? How will they find your product?

SOLVE THE PROBLEM

People get anxious when someone mentions a problem they have. This is where narrative comes into play in your marketing campaign. Present the problem in an inspirational way rather than an aggressive one.

Let's go back to the shampoo. Why use a commercial with stunning visuals and a delicate message? Because no one likes to be told their hair looks terrible. Imagine if the script was simply: "Horrible hair? Wash it with X shampoo."

GOALS

Set clear, specific goals for your campaigns. For example: This campaign will increase brand awareness; this one will drive sales; and this one will build brand loyalty. The more specific your goals are, the clearer your message will be, ultimately generating the results you want.

NO, TALENT ISN'T ENOUGH
TO BUILD AN AUDIENCE.
THERE'S MORE TO CULTIVATING
FOLLOWERS THAN BEING
GOOD AT SOMETHING.

BRANDING

It's time to talk about the culmination of the previous two topics—the intangible value of your life's work. Your brand.

Branding is how you make others feel when you aren't in the room. We've been discussing emotion and narrative in this cozy coffee shop, and I need you to know your brand is all of that wrapped into one. Every emotion you convey to your followers (or will convey, depending on where you are on your journey) will either elevate or diminish your brand. There's no running from the truth. We all have a personal brand, whether we're aware of it or not.

Here's a little tip to help you understand branding: Think of it as a personality. The first impression you have of someone. The way you're greeted when you first walk into a store. The joy when you try something new. Branding is feeling.

I can't tell you how many times I've worked with clients whose first obstacle was deconstructing the notion that the logo they designed was the crowning jewel of their entire brand.

Some proudly showed me what they created online, assets selected from an endless library because they looked good. If it were that simple, we wouldn't spend hours and hours poring over strategy, focus groups, and color studies so a visual asset can connect with its target audience.

Do you remember waking up on Christmas morning to gifts under the tree? Branding is the gorgeous giftwrap—the feeling you get before you've even seen what's inside.

Think about the fast-food restaurant that uses red and yellow in their logo. Are you seeing the arches? Now think of the first thing you felt when I painted that mental picture. *It's not the healthiest option, but it tastes good. It's cheap, and I'll be in and out of the drive-thru in less than five minutes.* Boom. Their branding is convenience, ease, and food.

You're at the mall and see a purse on display. It's black, sleek, exclusive. You hold it in your hands and imagine yourself out and about with that purse. You're walking into meetings, going out to dinner, and conducting business while wearing it. You feel powerful. Boom. Branding.

You walk inside a bookstore in search of a new read. You look through the shelves until you see a cover that catches your eye. The font, title, and visuals evoke the feeling of adventure you're after. You read the blurb, flip through the first chapter, and imagine yourself with the book on a beach or in your favorite reading corner. Boom. Branding. I don't care what others say, we all judge books by their covers. If you're in search of a rom-com and see a book with a severed head on the cover, you wouldn't even consider picking it up.

Branding is the conduit of emotion. It's what you can't touch or see that is the most important factor when purchasing a product or having someone become part of your audience. Just remember, a strong brand has the power to not only inspire purchases, but everlasting loyalty.

At the ripe age of fifteen, I started taking on freelance graphic design work. And as I designed a myriad of assets for clients of different backgrounds and nationalities, I observed a few patterns. Even if the client didn't connect with what they saw right away, it was how I presented the work, the way I conducted the meeting, and how I approached the overall project that put a price tag on it.

People will pay a lot more if you can make them feel. What makes you go back to a restaurant is not only the food, but the way you were greeted, the memories you have with the people you love, the way you felt when you were sitting at that table on a first date.

When I'm at my place in New Jersey, I like to make my own coffee in the morning. But as soon as I set foot in Massachusetts, I rush to Dunkin' and place my usual order: a cappuccino with almond milk and a plain toasted bagel with cream cheese. Suddenly, I am a teenager again, grabbing coffee with my friends after school. When I see the bubbly letters and orange color, my mind goes to my childhood days. And it feels good to be back there for a while.

When my family moved to America, my father's first job was as a baker at a Dunkin' in Framingham. During my first year, I would constantly call and ask him to bring pastries and drinks home.

But we have to be honest, coffee is coffee. Whether it's Dunkin', Starbucks, or a local brewer, the product is the same and the qualities are similar. What makes us prefer one over the other are the feelings we get when we consume them, their environment, or even the cup design.

BRANDING IS HOW YOU
MAKE OTHERS FEEL WHEN
YOU AREN'T IN THE ROOM.

BRANDING
VIA ASSOCIATION

We've all seen them. Celebrities out and about sporting particular purses, shoes, or cars. And suddenly, it's everywhere. Everyone wants to drive it. Everyone wants to wear it. Everyone wants it. The photos make it seem as if they were simply going about their day with a product that will soon be desired by many. Chances are, whatever brand they are wearing will increase in both value and profit. The product will fly off the shelves in days (if not hours) after they are seen.

How about famous people in beauty commercials? Recognizable faces on fragrance posters? Why do brands insist on featuring them in campaigns? Branding via association. It's the secret to elevating a brand's value and reaching a new audience fast. These brands leverage the feelings evoked by the personalities they hire.

One that immediately comes to mind is Timothée Chalamet for Chanel. Why would Chanel spend millions on a 90-second commercial and bring in Martin Scorsese to direct it? Why is the narrative for a cologne campaign about finding who you are?

Because by associating Bleu to Timothée, Chanel positioned its infamous fragrance on a blank canvas, ready to paint a new picture.

Millennials are very familiar with the previous face of the cologne, Johnny Depp. We grew up watching his movies. To millennials, he was known as Jack Sparrow, Sweeney Todd, and the Mad Hatter. To Gen Z and A, he is a controversial figure tied to scandal after scandal. His characters come second.

I attended a talk by David Grutman in 2022. His session was brief, but in the time he had, he taught the audience about the importance of this matter. He elevated his business and image by being seen with strategic people. I clearly remember him saying, "But what does being seen with a basketball player or influencer have to do with hospitality?"

Association. Suddenly, the head of a hospitality business was hanging out with the most influential personalities in Hollywood. This isn't to say honest friendships and relationships weren't born through this endeavor. I'd like to think so. But the truth was that he was intentional about what was made public.

Audiences think like this: *Oh, if John is associating with Mary and ensuring the public knows about it, he must like her. Let's research her. The probability that we might like Mary as well is high.*

Association heightens feelings, which is the primary reason brands collab with personalities or other brands. Whether it's clothes, books, or coffee, we use brands as a form of self-expression. It's no longer about the shoe, but the shoe *after* someone of influence has worn it.

Here are a few collaborations that are still ingrained in our minds: Kim Kardashian for Balenciaga, Nike and Michael Jordan, and Gucci x Disney. For the good or ill of these brands, their campaigns are memorable, becoming targets of inspiration and discourse.

Association ensures we give people a task they love to do. Talk. Talk about the good and the controversial.

In the same way we take risks on relationships, brands and companies take risks with associations.

Being the topic of conversation asserts a position of power. An entire project can soar to new heights or fall into the deepest pits because of the brand and people involved.

Association isn't just about a face. It's about the audience following that face and brand. Values and messages are joined before the public.

Think with me. If you get married, depending on your arrangement, you share assets. Association works the same way. You share brand equity and audience expansion.

An example is the partnership between Havaianas and Dolce & Gabbana. If you grew up in Brazil, you are no stranger to Havaianas. The flip-flops were created and made famous in the sixties. To this day, they're the most worn sandals in the country. To position themselves in the luxury market, Havaianas and Dolce & Gabbana joined forces to create an exclusive collection. The flip-flops for the campaign featured Havaianas' classic design and Dolce's very recognizable patterns. On the sole of the flip-flops, "Dolce & Gabbana & Havaianas" was printed.

A product already famous in the market was immediately elevated to the luxury consumer. *If Dolce hearts it, then I will try it.*

Brand association does come with a set of risks. Balenciaga's 2022 campaign had everyone talking. I am still confused as to how pictures of children holding harnessed teddy bears were reviewed, approved, and made public without anyone thinking, *Wow, this will get people riled up.* The campaign forced Kim Kardashian (who'd been very public about her love for the brand) to speak out.

All public figures are held accountable by their audiences. I understand the need for privacy. God, we all need it. But there are certain moments when creators must speak out about situations that affect their personal brand and message.

Values matter in association. People judge. You are essentially a cover, and people will judge who you associate with.

Let me speak from personal experience. Growing up evangelical, I was often told not to engage with "worldly people" (come on, are the rest of us from Mars?) in certain places because, if seen, members of the church would think you were backsliding. For those unfamiliar, "backsliding" in Christian terms pertains to someone who's falling away from the Christian faith.

Let's analyze the situation for a second. What is *actually* taking place is they believe your association with someone outside of their norm sends a mixed signal. How can someone of the faith be seen having a drink at a gay bar without raising questions?

Imagine I am a religious speaker, and I post a picture of myself at a sex shop. Who's to say religious speakers don't buy sex toys? Everyone should live their best lives, but it'd be foolish to ignore the unwanted associations a picture like that would have on the speaker's brand.

People wouldn't initially think, *Wow, this man is really enjoying the pleasures the Lord has given him.* Or *He and his wife must have a pretty steamy time in the bedroom.*

Most likely, the first thoughts would be of scandal and shock. *There's no need to make their sex lives public.* Even though most of us have sex.

Brand association when building a business is crucial. So be clever when making things public. What you put out there belongs to the world, and people have the power to either agree or criticize it.

We have reached immortality in the digital age. What we share today will last years to come. Many individuals are seeking anonymity because content will outlast us all. If you are a creative entrepreneur, do not treat your online channels like a private diary.

Here's a little nugget to help you. Whenever you decide to make something public, think about these three things: 1) Is this an investment on people's perception of my brand? 2) If people agree with my message, how will this resonate with me in the future? 3) How will haters react?

Entrepreneurs must be ready for these scenarios and learn how to leverage them. Calculate your footsteps. Be mindful of them. Feelings are not excuses. Don't share something simply because you feel like it. Intentionality is your best friend in the game of association.

That brings us to our next checkpoint. Take a moment and imagine your best friend. Who do you associate them with? You will soon see why that matters.

ASSOCIATION ENSURES WE GIVE PEOPLE A TASK THEY LOVE TO DO. TALK. TALK ABOUT THE GOOD AND THE CONTROVERSIAL.

THE CIRCLE

There's no point in time for the invention of the circle. It's always been around. The wheel eventually joined the scene—and with it, the ability to move at a much faster rate than before. Carriages, cars, mobility.

I am calling this part of our conversation "the circle," not only to describe the people around us, but as a mirror to the environment's power to propel us, stall us, or send us backward.

We've all heard it said that we are the equivalent of the people closest to us. Let me take this a step further. We are the equivalent of the books we read, the news we watch, the series we enjoy. We are responsible for the relationships and sources we allow into our lives.

One of my favorite pastimes is watching animal videos. I've stumbled upon a few that left me thinking. Videos of ducks who believe they are chickens, and dogs who try to move like the kids they play with. Though they are very funny, I can't help but think many of us suffer the same fates. Perhaps that duck will go its entire life without enjoying any duck-ish shenanigans because it will always believe it was meant to scratch at the ground instead of flying or swimming in ponds. Or the dog will think itself a failure for walking on four legs when, in actuality, it is exceptional.

We are often less ourselves and do less than we can because we are surrounded by the wrong crowd. Like nature, we evolve with time and require different landscapes to thrive.

While we share the same planet with an array of beings, we are each our own universes. And we must be mindful of those who are given a pass to reside in our spaces. We cannot influence with honesty if our circle doesn't reflect that.

But J.D., why are we talking about ducks and chickens in a conversation about branding? Because branding is also about the company we keep. I can't emphasize enough the importance of curating your circle. Your personal brand will either soar or be diminished because of every component that plays a part in it.

Brilliant projects fail because people choose the wrong members for their circles. And worse, they don't have the guts to kick them out, afraid they'll hurt them.

I am not encouraging you to be an ass. I am encouraging you to stand up for *yourself* so you can be in an environment that inspires your way forward. People waste years of their lives doing what they hate because they are afraid of other people's opinions and perceptions.

When you become a doer, you attract wishers—those who long to be as bold or adventurous. I am okay with people wanting something from me. We all want something in the end.

We like Mary because she's fun. We love John because he is great to talk to. I want to get closer to Steven Spielberg because he might read one of my stories and decide to adapt it. You want the job because it'll give you new opportunities.

A thriving circle is observed *and* envied. While some add to the journey, others come for the taking. There is no running from it. Sometimes, I am good at spotting these individuals. Other times, they find their way in without raising a single red flag. Instead of punishing myself for my lack of perception, I let them do what they want.

I see an opportunity—lessons and observations I'll carry for a lifetime. When I realize I am in control, I let them run wild. Yes, *I* let them. I observe patterns of behavior that teach me to be a better creative entrepreneur—the way they talk and act, the words they use. I never let my guard down, but I allow them to think I did.

In the book *The 48 Laws of Power* by Robert Greene, the author mentions the law of concealing your intentions. Hide your true intentions while leading those who seek to take advantage down the wrong path. Keep them guessing. They won't have much else to do but leave once they realize what you did.

A circle is inspiration and protection, but also a teacher. Observe wisely, and you will learn without pain. Miss a step, and you will learn surrounded by empathy.

PEOPLE WASTE YEARS OF THEIR LIVES DOING WHAT THEY HATE BECAUSE THEY ARE AFRAID OF OTHER PEOPLE'S OPINIONS AND PERCEPTIONS.

THE CHARACTERS
IN YOUR STORY

Listen, I can't even pretend to not thoroughly enjoy this part of our conversation. Creating characters that will populate, live, and die in my own universes brings me great joy.

You may have heard of the 10,000-hour rule made popular by Malcolm Gladwell. To make it simple, you need to have spent 10,000 hours at something to be qualified. I've been drawing, designing, and writing for as long as I can remember. And I've been creating characters for even longer.

But characters can't exist without an ecosystem of their own. And stories can't exist without an audience's reaction and immersion. Both story and worldbuilding are required in the game of narrative (fantasy or otherwise). During my childhood, I'd lock myself in my bedroom with pen and paper, pop in a cassette of the *Titanic* or *Jurassic Park* soundtrack, and write and draw for hours. I'd come up with the wildest stories. From superheroes getting lost on a safari to a ghost ship sinking in scorching waters to a pair of lovers being eaten by dinosaurs. Seeing my characters breathe life into the worlds I created reassured me of what I wanted to do with my life.

Creating characters is a joyful and therapeutic experience for me. As a writer who works in multiple genres, I can say with confidence that no matter how epic the story, readers will *always* connect with the humanity behind each character.

I'm sure you're no stranger to stories, shows, and movies with mythical creatures. Let's take dragons for instance. They are fierce characters and nearly insurmountable beasts. I know I'm not the only one who feels a little pain in my heart when the dragon dies in the middle of a raging battle.

Whether magical or ordinary, coming up with a character's strengths, weaknesses, and personalities requires creativity, and…are you ready? Research. In media, characters hold monetary value, and the more an audience connects to them, the more they are worth. Sure, superpowers and special abilities are fantastic, but it's their courage, brokenness, and wickedness that makes them relatable. No character can be perfect, because perfection is boring and predictable. The most colorful characters are often the most interesting, thus captivating audiences the longest.

In recent years, the most memorable books and shows feature characters we both root for and constantly question. As a society, we have evolved from a black-and-white point of view to a multi-layered perspective. This evolution also applies to consumers.

The art of creating characters requires an analysis of the human psyche—a deep dive into our wins, losses, needs, and pain. Every story requires emotional depth. The same can be applied when researching the characters who will populate your personal ecosystem—the ones who will talk your brand up, disagree with you, and question you. You want to create worlds for all of them. Yes, even your most gray characters need an environment to thrive in so you can be rewarded for their actions—no matter how questionable.

I was very intentional when I wrote *The Echoes of Fallen Stars: Immortal Crowns.* The book was an artistic expression, sure, but in the context of business, I wanted to create a product that was both shocking, thought-provoking, and poetic. I was ready for a new audience—one that expected bolder moves.

For those not familiar with my fallen angel fantasy, the series is a retelling of the Creator/Lucifer story. We follow Bellwound, Lucifer's lost son, living an ordinary life in a remote village. He is secretly in love with his childhood friend Arnon. When visited by a Nephilin, Bellwound discovers his parents were secret keepers of Lucifer's epistle. He sets out on a journey to protect this sacred device, only to discover that Lucifer and the Creator were lovers before they became enemies.

You either scrunched up your face or smirked at that description. But you had a reaction regardless. These books were meant to do just that—evoke a reaction that would make them memorable. I wanted them to tell my current and future audience I am a bold creator.

I was no stranger to the possibility of backlash. I leveraged it. The more people talked about the books, the more the intended audience grew interested. A few months later, Dreamscape Lore bought the audio rights for the series. A year later, the cover of the second book was plastered on the Nasdaq billboard in Times Square. I knew the feature would generate press. Lo and behold, there was both good press and some questionable mentions.

During release week, I received a call from a reporter known for his articles in a certain Republican news outlet. While questioning me about book bans and queerness in storytelling, he asked for my thoughts on the drop in intellectual property (IP) profitability when queer characters were front and center.

Paraphrasing, my response was something along the lines of, "I can't speak on a studio's profitability regarding their IP, but I can say that had I seen queer characters represented as heroes, I would've saved thousands in therapy."

I expected characters like him to pop into the world I'd created. I wanted them to, actually. I designed an entire arc so people like him would do what I intended them to do. These books were my way of exploring extreme acceptance and criticism. There's no in-between for these books. They are either really loved or really hated.

Apply that principle to creative entrepreneurship. Your business-slash-brand is the world you are building. What world-building is to novels, branding and narrative is to entrepreneurship. You need your players. You need your main character—the one who will carry the torch, the embodiment of everything you stand for and against.

Every good story needs supporting characters. Not everyone can be in the spotlight at once. Otherwise, the audience becomes confused. Let me give you a hand in understanding these characters and how they play a role in your brand's narrative.

THE ANTAGONIST

You've got to love good opposition in a story. In real life? Maybe not so much. But whether you like it or not, you will need to create a place for your antagonists. If you can predict their moves and anticipate their behavior, you will reap the benefits of your audience's judgement.

I'm going to assume you're no stranger to Taylor Swift. Regardless of how you feel about her music, she has built an empire by anticipating how her audience will react (both admirers and haters). The press criticizes her for dating too much? Here's new music with a narrative of empowerment. Critics say her music is bland? Here's a new album with twenty songs and countless special editions. Oh, they said she was a snake? Here's an entire era around the snake archetype. Fans root for her. Critics talk about her. Haters build her up. And her empire grows.

THE BACKGROUND CHARACTERS

You know those people you text and never get a reply from, but you see them on your social media? Well, say hello to your background characters. They are there for numbers and likes, but don't expect an honest reaction from them. They may congratulate you on an achievement and like something you share, but they'll never actually attend an event or consume anything you put out.

They have their place. Keep them as followers and in your newsletters. Having them in your rolodex only adds to how expansive your network is. And don't take their actions to heart..

In the same way a message needs a messenger, a company or brand needs people to grow. Get good at observing them and their behaviors without immediate judgement. If you can be more intentional anout how you react when it comes to the actions and reactions of people, you will slowly and naturally be able to flesh out the characters for your own brand's narrative.

EVERY STORY NEEDS SUPPORTING
CHARACTERS. NOT EVERYONE
CAN BE IN THE SPOTLIGHT
AT ONCE.

MASTER
YOUR CRAFT

From an early age, I knew I wanted to be the boss of my own life and career. While that's a beautiful sentiment, the reality is you need money to get the ball rolling.

I'll never forget the first time I made money from graphic design work. I was a fifteen-year-old high schooler, and my mom had come home talking about a friend who needed a business card designed. While I was happy to get the gig, I struggled to design it, spending hours on something that should have taken a fraction of the time.

Right after school, I'd eat, take a quick shower, and get dropped off at Shopper's World for my job at Marshalls. I realized that if I wanted to design faster, I needed to invest in my skills. The little bit of money I made went toward buying online courses. While the household was asleep, I'd stay up learning to create layers, work with typography, the difference between RGB and CMYK, and so on.

A light bulb went off in my head. No matter the industry, everyone needs graphic design (unless a company wants to stay in the dark ages). I became obsessed with designing posters inspired by bands I loved and sharing them in blog posts online. Suddenly, I had people looking forward to my work. They wanted to see more.

I'd walk around the city, looking for inspiration for my next post in movie posters, CD booklets, DVD inserts, and magazines. Everything was inspiration to get better at my craft.

It was on one of my walks that I stumbled across a local print shop that was Brazilian-owned. I walked right up to the owner and started talked about my graphic design abilities. When I showed my little blog, I was offered the role of junior designer. Since I attended a technical school, I had the chance to work full-time and finish junior and senior year together. All I had to do was prove to my school that I could still manage my assignments. And I did just that.

A couple of years and a move to Florida later, I was invited to work at a luxury real estate firm in Brickell. During that time, I was living about forty-five minutes north of Miami. It was quite the commute, and I was hesitant about taking the job. But I came up with a plan.

I had just finished writing my first novel. Working full-time at the real estate firm would give me exposure, a prestigious network, and the funds to hone my writing and design skills. There's nothing wrong with having a 9-to-5. When you're starting out, it's the 9-to-5 that will bring in the seed money needed to invest in your craft. We don't pay bills with well-wishes after all.

I've been seeing more and more influencers build their messages around their 9-to-5s. Not everyone dreams of being a creative entrepreneur. And that's totally fine. But there's one truth that applies to us all—we will keep mastering our crafts until the day we die.

You may achieve stardom. You may be the next big thing. You may one day fill stadiums and release timeless songs. You'll still need to improve the skills you already have.

I am proud of the young adult in me who had the guts to release his first novel. If I read that book today, I'd appreciate my growth as a writer and storyteller. I have a box with my early graphic design work—brochures, magazines, and cards I designed for clients over a decade ago. I can see my growth when I look at those pieces.

Fast forward to the present. If I were to read the books I've released in the past three years, I'd still find areas where I can be stronger. I listen back to my public speeches and make note of the places I need to improve.

A new social media platform will drop. A new web design platform will be created. New entrepreneurial tools will be made. We will always need to grow in our craft.

Constantly honing your craft means staying relevant. Adaptability is required if you want to be better at what you do.

What worked ten years ago in some industries will not work now. I remember when social media used to deliver content to our followers without a curated algorithm. You followed someone and you saw their posts. Today, if you do not understand the algorithms and media-buying strategies, your content becomes obsolete.

Honing your craft is also about being mindful of what you consume. If you're a financial advisor, read about your industry, watch videos, listen to podcasts. You bake? Then remember to take some time for yourself to learn new recipes and improve your skills.

As a designer, I am constantly keeping an eye out for new trends, reading magazines and books, and consuming media that inspires me to improve. As an author, I'm observing trends, behavior, and industry pivots so I can continue to write relevant tales. As a brand strategist, I am tracking the evolution of narrative and storytelling in society.

But there's one common denominator across all industries—one that will always be at the core of why brands are established. How are people behaving these days? And yes, I mean *how*. Within your industry, are they more inclined to swipe through graphics or watch short videos? Maybe they're not even online. Perhaps they consume printed media, and that's where your engagement will take place.

Your talent will take you far, but it's understanding how people feel that will keep you at the top of the game.

CONSTANTLY HONING
YOUR CRAFT MEANS STAYING
RELEVANT. ADAPTABILITY
IS REQUIRED IF YOU WANT
TO BE BETTER AT WHAT YOU DO.

THE GIFT
OF SILENCE

In an age where we curate our best moments before sharing them with the world, it's easy to confuse noise with progress.

Hustle culture has evolved from an isolated virus into a pandemic. Don't stop. Don't sleep. Work. Create. Work again. Down time? That's for the weak and lazy. We need to always be building something.

The issue with this reality is we're seeing people with incredible ideas get overwhelmed by the illusion of *doing* something rather than *building* a legacy.

J.D., are we still on topic here? Absolutely. In graphic design, there is something we call negative space. It's the empty areas around an element or text that lets the design breathe. Negative space brings clarity and order.

In the same way designs need to breathe, so do we. We need to be comfortable with the deep silences of our lives—the moments when we work in secret and no one is watching.

Let's be honest about something. It's become incredibly difficult to disconnect from our phones. And while they are an essential tool for business and connection, phones can also be the trigger that leads to procrastination and self-doubt.

Let me paint a picture. You're working on your side hustle—the one you hope will become your main gig. You need to disconnect for a bit, so you pick up your phone. The first thing you see is a twenty-something-year-old explaining why you should have a million dollars in the bank by the age of twenty-five. You keep scrolling, and another post will tell you the economy is collapsing, and you shouldn't start a business right now.

Suddenly, everyone feels incredibly productive. They're working tirelessly toward their goals and dreams. And you? You feel lazy, like a sloth resting on a branch while others are climbing or a tortoise left behind by minds racing towards brilliance faster than you.

You get immersed in online promises from accounts who have carefully curated every image, every word, and every piece of dialogue to spark a certain emotion in you. But it doesn't stop there. The picture of the perfect couple, the friend in Europe, your favorite influencer dressed in an expensive brand.

What we fail to realize is every person crafted a careful narrative with their posts. We don't see the *why* behind the *what*. So instead of analyzing our own narrative, we resort to reactive behavior. *I can't be left behind. I need to show the world I'm working toward something.*

You search for a picture or video that will let you be a part of the club. You can't remain in the shadows when everyone is in the spotlight. You give in to the emotion. You don't plan your content. You simply share something. Vanity becomes the enemy of intentionality.

I've been a victim of this myself. While working in my own private creative haven, I am hit with content from others making progress. I feel like an imposter, needing my audience's sudden validation.

Herein lies the bigger issue. You see. You post. You scroll. You compare.

Not a lot is shared about the power of remaining silent. The truth is, we get to control our absences, and there's power in not being seen. Absence stirs conversation. *I wonder what they've been up to?*

The statement, "out of sight, out of mind" may ring true, but what you see too often can become cheap and tiring.

I had a friend ask why I became more selective of what I shared on my socials. My response was simple, "I want people to get excited when I share something, not used to the sharing."

You get too many emails from a company, and you block them. Too many releases from your favorite artist, and you lose the excitement. Too many calls, and you get tired.

Silence sets the tone for a reset, building anticipation for what comes next.

This is by no means an excuse to not put in the work when an opportunity arises. This is more about the need for immediate gratification and giving a play-by-play instead of a finished result. Our desire for validation becomes the enemy of creation.

When I first started writing, I did so for the simple joy of the story. My first book took me six years to complete. I had no intention of ever publishing it. I was just experimenting with an idea I had. No one knew I was writing a book, so it was quite the surprise when I finally revealed it. I noticed the sudden respect I garnered, even though I hadn't published it yet.

Of course, once I got published, I had a contract and deadlines to meet. Even today, I find myself in scenarios where I must remind myself of the power of silence.

Silence sets the tone for wondering and allows people to create their own narratives. So many artists use silence to their advantage. Adele drops an album, tours, then disappears for years. Do I need to talk about Rihanna? How about George R.R. Martin? Will he ever finish *A Song of Ice and Fire*?

It'd be foolish to change the topic of conversation and not mention the pressures we are under when it comes to content creation. No matter your area of expertise, everyone is creating content to stay relevant and not get pushed out by the algorithm. While this is a relatively new shift we've all had to embrace, remember that trends come and go. Adapt but *do not* settle.

IN AN AGE WHERE WE CURATE
OUR BEST MOMENTS BEFORE
SHARING THEM WITH
THE WORLD, IT'S EASY
TO CONFUSE NOISE
WITH PROGRESS.

WHEN YOU ARE
NOT IN THE ROOM

The reality is people's perceptions of you take place even when you are not in the room. That is a fact. People talk. That is *also* a fact. Whether you are around to hear it or not, someone, somewhere is talking about you. And I don't mean gossip. This isn't your family sitting in a living room somewhere discussing your life. This is about your potential clients, your network, your customers, your audience.

Embracing the fact that people will always have something to say gives you control over the narrative. And no, this isn't manipulation. It's about nurturing inspiration.

What happens the moment we consume a good product or have an incredible experience? We talk. We talk to friends, family, and social media followers. It's in our nature to share.

The same applies to terrible experiences. In 2014, right after my first book signing in New York City, I decided to go to an early dinner to celebrate with friends. We found this Italian restaurant in SoHo that had rave reviews. They promised homemade pasta, drinks, the works.

The four of us sat down and the waiter brought menus. My friend and I were so thrilled when we realized we could add shrimp to our pasta that we ordered without looking at the price. We expected to pay extra for the shrimp, but not seventy-five dollars each!

The price jumped out at us seconds—I kid you not—seconds after the waiter walked away. When we asked to change the order, we were told no. I stared at the man deadpan, thinking of a million things I could say. But we were celebrating. I'd just had my first signing in New York, and it was a sold-out event. I was willing to let it slide. The pasta was going to be fresh and the homemade sauce…

My friend and I made peace with the disaster. Until we decided to wage war. When I tell you that pasta was frozen and the shrimp undercooked. It is still the most disappointing meal of my life.

It's been ten years, and I have never returned to that restaurant. When friends visit New York from out of town, I tell them to steer clear of the place.

The restaurant decided to stand by their cold food and not refund the money. But I am quite sure they didn't expect their actions to still be leaking into conversations years later. I might tell you which restaurant it is if you shoot me a DM. We'll see. Even this conversation is happening while they are not in the room—it's just you and me.

Trying to control other people's narratives of you leads to madness. That's not the point here. The point is to be intentional about the experience people have *with* your brand. What do you want them to say when you aren't in the room?

If people are going to love what you're putting out, you need to have a solid plan for audiences embracing your message. What will they get out of your narrative? What narrative will you continue to write so they remain engaged? If you want to create something that will stir the pot, create a path for both constructive and destructive criticism.

Anticipating these actions will create opportunities for your brand to travel farther than you can. Make no mistake. Marketing campaigns are not built on good press alone. Criticism can be a massive strategy for growth.

Always think of the opposition and what they'll say when you aren't around. How will they inspire others to seek you out? And what will this new audience see once they find you?

Campaigns for politicians are built on this principal. Scandal leads to curiosity. Criticism generates clicks. As a result, there's exponentially more traffic searching for a certain person or theme.

I have heard of politicians whose teams create extremely detailed campaigns against themselves. They bet on the topics that will generate the most discord and buzz.

Rest assured, the reactions we have toward their videos, ads, or articles is exactly what is expected of us. Controversy runs faster than any other message.

No, we don't have to agree with scandal, but it is true. This isn't an encouragement to create something so obscene your current or future audience won't resonate with you. This is an invitation to the whiteboard of creativity.

Let's say your brand is about empowering certain communities. The community supporting you will rally behind your message while the opposition will stir discord. Anticipate what they'll say and do. Imagine the most relevant scenarios for both. Ask yourself, how can I benefit from their actions at the end of the day?

THE REALITY IS PEOPLE'S
PERCEPTIONS OF YOU
TAKE PLACE EVEN WHEN
YOU ARE NOT IN THE ROOM.

Whether you're building a brand, launching a product, or are simply curious about the subject, the word "no" is your best friend.

One of the shortest words in the English language is one of the most feared—and one of the most misused. So many of us see this word in a negative light, believing that wielding its power will somehow make us the worst of villains.

I used to be somewhat of a people pleaser. I discovered I had talent at a very young age. The artist in me loved the attention. Artists crave an audience after all. My talent made people feel something.

Music was another passion of mine, but it wasn't until my early teens that I decided to explore it. I'd watch my friend playing keyboard and wonder how he knew what combination of keys would make such beautiful music. After a few classes, I learned the basics of the instrument and ran with my gift. Singing came after

Church played a big role in my life in my teenage years. There was a lot of validation from that kind of community if you had a talent that could be used on stage. I was looking for validation, as all teenagers do, and found it in religion.

While I was meant to be leading folks into Godly praise through my performances, I got praised for how I made them feel. I started saying yes to whatever got me noticed in that circle.

The church leadership demanded artists be a public example of obedience. In a very passive aggressive way, we were encouraged to attend as many church events as possible. Whenever I or other key musicians were absent from one of those events, the leadership made sure to mention how lacking the music sets were. I was a volunteer, but in my fear of saying no, I took on a burden that didn't belong to me.

I said yes to playing at many services and events. In the back of my mind, I thought I was saying yes to "serving the Lord." I believe a part of me held on to that truth because another was reminding me that being on the music team wasn't my job.

I found it interesting to observe people's reactions when little ol' church me started saying no. Suddenly, I was a rebel, and the more I said no, the more I started seeing what that particular community was all about.

We often get caught in loops of failure because we aren't comfortable declining requests. Blame it on your upbringing, religion, or friends, but if we are here at this coffee shop having this conversation, you are old enough to stop blaming the world and start looking into yourself.

In a world where the lost say yes, be one of the bold who say no. The word "no" is a life-changing tool that is barely used. "No" isn't offensive. "No" asserts that you are not for everybody. You can't build anything of true meaning without learning when to say this word. Goals require constant nos.

I moved to the New York City area in 2021 and soon realized that if I said yes to every single opportunity the city offered, I'd be lost in a sea of constant people-pleasing. It's another thing to network and say yes to what truly fulfills you. Hence the reason why we started this conversation with self-reflection and discovery.

You don't become successful in your craft or savvy in your industry because of your yeses. It's your nos that make others respect you.

One thing I love about this concept is that filtering out your life by declining what no longer suits you shows the reality of your surroundings. Those who respect you will praise you for being so steady in what you believe.

Learning to be comfortable with your nos can be scary. You spiral and create a million scenarios for how people will perceive you when you decline requests. I was once offered a chairman position for a very influential leadership group. The brand of the group had suffered great damage due to past leadership. Their approach was cunning. They needed a new face and a breath of fresh air so the brand could connect with younger minds. The position would also place me in front of certain leaders and entrepreneurs that could potentially bring in business.

The catch? They had to be my top priority. I'd have to lead an entire team, pay for the name usage (which I found absurd), and work on a campaign of brand reinvigoration pro bono before making a profit. Sure, the potential for what was to come seemed profitable, but my yes would've led me away from the goals and ambitions I already had.

They questioned my decision to decline. It was their right to do so. As it was mine to stand my ground.

The narrative people write about you in their minds isn't your problem. Stay on course—say yes to what makes sense and no to what doesn't.

THE NARRATIVE PEOPLE
WRITE ABOUT YOU
IN THEIR MINDS ISN'T
YOUR PROBLEM.

THE EMOTIONAL
HOOK

We all love a good story. Times change, and we still cling to characters whose destinies unravel through trials and ordeals. There are three sides to every character: who they are, who they think they are, and who others think they are. To engage with your audience, you must create a powerful emotional bond through your characters and narrative

To no one's surprise, human beings go through tough times. No matter your status or background, things can get rocky here and there.

It's a lot easier to embrace what we are good at than to look at our flaws and say, "I like those just as much." But I want to plant a little seed in your brain, a quote to help you make peace with your tough seasons: Perfection is the enemy of connection.

The hero archetype has been around for thousands of years. No matter how many stories we consume, we still get butterflies when the hero fulfills their purpose.

But there's no good story without ups and downs. If the hero's journey was all about the ups, we'd have a flat plot—one without a chance of connecting with an audience.

Think about your favorite book or movie. The main character is probably an outsider, someone who wishes they had a bigger purpose. Or its someone who wants to remain anonymous, but the bigger purpose finds them. Fast forward to the end, and it is the contrast between their roots and achievements that makes them earn their crown.

Narratives evolve like fashion and music. We are shying away from the black and white and embracing the gray. We all know that every action has a reaction. Let me add to it. For every action, there is a motivation.

Narratives in the 80s and 90s relied a lot on the good guy and the bad guy. The good guy was pure light, and the bad guy was darkness. In recent times, we find ourselves enveloped in stories where characters have more depth. They are more complex. Audiences crave backstories.

It isn't so much about the villain or the hero, but about the motivation behind their actions. Some are twisted and some are justified. But all in all, audiences want the stability of the narrative and the surprise of the plot.

The Greeks excelled at the craft of writing gray characters. Zeus was unfaithful and vengeful while being the ultimate creator. Dionysius was a symbol for chaos and ecstasy. The list goes on and on. And we are still drawing inspiration from those stories today.

This isn't an invitation to be as wild as the Greek gods. This is inspiration for you to embrace all sides of your narrative and share the parts that will strengthen your platform.

Not everyone will follow a brand on socials, but audiences will follow a brand's founder. Audiences crave the journey. They'll connect with your humble—or not-so-humble—beginnings, the ladders you climbed, and the tough conversations you had.

I'll start.

Two weeks after my twelfth birthday, my family moved to the United States. During my first summer, I read all the books on my school's reading list. I wanted to immerse myself in the culture as much as I could because, even at a young age, I knew my immigrant story would set me apart.

As the years passed, I realized keeping my Brazilian culture alive at home while having an American education and upbringing allowed me to connect effectively with both worlds.

In my twenties, many Brazilian entrepreneurs sought out my expertise in branding and design because of my dual mindset. My circumstances might have led many to believe I wouldn't achieve half of what I did. We came on a tourist visa seeking a better life, with no meaningful connections or monetary power in America. I am a product of divorce. But still, I took a chance on myself.

See what I did there? What you just read is true, but now my work and who I have become has more value and meaning because of my strife.

Immigrant stories can be seen as weaknesses by immigrants themselves. As a Brazilian-American, I can attest to this truth within my community. When I was a kid, the common phrase I'd hear was, "It's a hard-earned life." I never liked that affirmation. "Earn" implies a painful sacrifice. I believe it's a life you build.

Building requires tools, and that's exactly what you have in your toolbox. Whether you come from a faceless or famous family, your emotional hook is tied to your hurdles and achievements.

Narrative cannot be bought. It must be written through experience. A few famous people may have crossed your mind—people with fortunes and miserable lives. Some will frown at your struggles. I bet you did the moment I said "famous." Because we immediately think, *That isn't a struggle. That's privilege.* See how an emotional hook leads an audience to action?

Another example is the strong emotional connection religion has. Death results in life, belief results in ostracizing others, and the bended knees of the privileged keep the wheels turning. Religion thrives in the morally grey. The complex interplay between the saved and the damned built a massive global community that has lasted millennia. It's probably the most well-executed marketing campaign in history.

Let's wrap up this part of the conversation with an exercise. Feel free to use the space below, a notebook, or your notes app. On the left, write your emotional hooks: immigrant, minority, the peculiarities that make you stand out. On the right, for every emotional hook, describe the audience you'd like to reach. This exercise will serve as a confidence boost—a way to use your struggles as a strategy to build meaningful connections.

Cheers to the broken parts in us, folks!

Undocumented immigrant — aspiring entrepreneurs who have no papers

____

____

____

____

____

____

____

____

____

____

____

FOR EVERY ACTION,
THERE IS A MOTIVATION.

CHARACTER
OVER TALENT

Even as a kid, I noticed my talent was a way to start conversations. Whether through my drawings or the books I wrote, I caught and rode the wave of opportunity that came with my abilities.

Talent, of course, gives you an ego boost. And I don't know if anyone's ever mentioned this to you, but a healthy dose of ego does wonders for the soul. Since ego is our sense of self, a look inward makes space for a healthy relationship between the outside world and the one within.

The world is always abuzz when it discovers new talent. Whether it's a speaker, singer, or entrepreneur, there's an excitement about the shiny new toy. But like any other children's toy, what was once shiny eventually becomes ordinary.

Your talent might put you ahead of the game, but it won't let you play for long if you don't live up to the hype. And I don't mean the hype of how good you might be. I mean the hype of how great of a human you are.

Ego and talent walk hand in hand. One strokes the other, and that's the circle of life for any creative entrepreneur. Everyone likes being praised for their achievements. But once an audience has grown used to the new product, they'll remember our character and who we are at the core more than what made us money.

Let me paint you a picture. You finally land a big client after many calls and meetings. They've fallen in love with your portfolio and can't wait to start working on the project. Two weeks later, when you emerge from the pile of deadlines, you'll be remembered for how effectively you delivered the assets. Your talent will be in the back of your client's mind.

People get used to how good you are at your craft. How many singers release albums that flop because of a PR crisis? They're still good singers. They don't have to remind the world they can belt out hits. The world knows. Audiences come back for the story that unfolds with a new project—the reinvention of an artist's humanity during a season in their lives. And if that story is polluted by actions that display an unhealthy amount of ego, then guess what? The audience will most likely walk away or simply ignore the project altogether.

I've met many creatives who lost projects despite being talented. They were incredible at their craft, but inconsistent with their emails, replies, and timelines. Talent without commitment leads to frustration.

I've worked with designers and creatives from all over the world. No matter how gifted they might be, if they lacked proper *human* etiquette or character, I'd simply inform them our partnership was over.

No one is patient enough to stay in the business of ego for too long. Talent has a lot more value when its vessel is a conduit of good habits.

And yes, life happens, and when it does, none of us are obligated to disclose our personal affairs to those we work with. But we can still be courteous and update our timeline as best we can so expectations can be realigned.

Your talent is the product, but your work etiquette is the packaging. In the same way trends evolve, we must do the same so our packaging stays relevant.

While speaking to a crowd at an event, I brought two shampoo bottle designs. One was very elegant, with neutral colors and delicate fonts. The other was bright, with bold type and not a lot of design nuance. I asked the crowd how much each product was worth. The elegant bottle was valued at triple the price of the other. The catch? Inside each was the very same product. No matter how talented you are, your personal label is the first thing people see and the one thing they will remember.

YOUR TALENT MIGHT PUT YOU AHEAD OF THE GAME, BUT IT WON'T LET YOU PLAY FOR LONG IF YOU DON'T LIVE UP TO THE HYPE. AND I DON'T MEAN THE HYPE OF HOW GOOD YOU MIGHT BE. I MEAN THE HYPE OF HOW GREAT OF A HUMAN YOU ARE.

CHAMELEONS

One of the most incredible abilities of any creative entrepreneur is adaptability. In a fast-evolving world, being comfortable with making new spaces your own will put you ahead while others fall behind.

I tend to get nostalgic for the early 2010s. I remember what it felt like to release my first book, to open my LLC, to host my first signing.

I'm not going to pretend certain changes on the platforms I loved didn't discourage me from creating content. For a while, I sulked. I complained and complained until I realized the time I spent complaining was time I could spend creating.

Symbology is one of my passions. Whether it's a logo for a client or a symbol for my story, an image's ability to carry an extensive message has always felt powerful.

While I tend to gravitate towards lions, dragons, and majestic birds, the chameleon (to no one's surprise) is the most inspiring muse in the matter of adaptability.

These little animals don't complain about the change of environment. Instead, they take on the visual characteristics of their surroundings while leveraging their strength.

Many animals and symbols reflect the outward nature of the creative entrepreneur, but I believe the chameleon reflects the heart. We must comfortably adapt to new environments while moving with precision.

Chameleons don't speed through their environment. They are cold-blooded, which means the environment regulates their temperature, much like entrepreneurs must acclimate to new trends and industry demands.

Life is full of ups and downs, but there are two things we can expect—death and change. We can't talk about adaptability without addressing this truth. Don't hold on to something so tightly you aren't willing to evolve.

Let me get candid with you. I thought my first book was going to grant me a certain level of success. *The Whispers of the Fallen* released during the rise of Bookstagram. For those who've never heard the term, it was a word used for the book community on Instagram. While one still exists on the platform, I will be the millennial who says nothing compares to the early 2010s. So many great names spread like wildfire back then: Veronica Roth, Cassandra Clare, Rick Riordan, etc. And I was sure *Whispers* was going to be as big as their titles.

I can be honest with myself and say that while I was rewarded for a lot of the effort I put into those books, they were drowned out by other stories. I'm not complaining. They sold thousands of copies around the world. People flocked to book events looking for the sequels. Google the books and you'll see an array of posts created by my readers.

But despite the platform those four books gave me, I couldn't ignore the universe's request for me to adapt as a storyteller, an entrepreneur, and as a person. That meant reading more, writing more, immersing myself in this universe, and being more in tune with who I am.

There are days when you don't want to adapt. Some new trend comes out or another app is released, and all you want to do is give up and say, "Fuck it." We're people. Our feelings matter. Our exhaustions and frustrations matter. They deserve space, but some of them deserve a quick visit and a nice goodbye. Adaptability is linked to purpose. And when your purpose is tied to your mission, you become unstoppable.

Adaptability and honesty walk hand in hand. It isn't humiliating to sit with yourself and count your rewards and losses. Over the past decade, we've been trained to edit our lives for the internet. We talk about our achievements without mentioning the hurdles. We pretend life is a crystal-clear lake when it's actually an ever-changing, torrential river.

Value each stage in the past, present, and future. Never think you're so good that you no longer need to adapt. It's through change that we fuel our growth and success.

ADAPTABILITY AND
HONESTY WALK HAND
IN HAND. IT ISN'T HUMILIATING
TO SIT WITH YOURSELF
AND COUNT YOUR
REWARDS AND LOSSES.

JUDGEMENT AS RESEARCH

One of the most common ways to pass time is by scrolling. We all do it—no matter how much we might loathe it. Resorting to social media in search of dopamine has become a common habit. Most times, we don't even notice we're doing it.

Here and there, we stumble upon a few accounts that leave us talking. Whether it's a cute puppy video, an influencer who over-uses filters, or a video from a political party you disagree with, we judge and criticize.

This is in no way, shape, or form a validation of online hate. Disliking someone's content is not an excuse to spew insults in comments or private messages. People get to share whatever they want to share, but we don't get to say whatever we want to say. Un-fortunately, some are incapable of grasping that concept, but their behavior can be used to our advantage.

On a perfect planet, we'd be frolicking through eternal fields of magic, eating berries, and chasing waterfalls. But we live in a complicated world. People love together and fight for justice together. Discord and disagreement also create community. People can find like-minded folks with a vein of what they dislike connecting them.

One of my first projects was designing this gorgeous brochure for a spa. I spent hours on the typography, design elements, copy, and imagery. When the time came for me to present it to the client, I was flooded with questions that picked apart what I had created.

My books solidified that lesson. Though I was offered a scholarship at the time, I couldn't attend college due to my status in the US. That didn't stop me from learning, but it did make me more vulnerable since I had to do so in the public eye of thousands of readers.

Those books are a reflection of my learning years, but readers didn't know that. I gave them a story and, with it, the freedom to review my work. It was a struggle to shake off my frustrations whenever a negative review was posted online. Whatever praise my work received was overshadowed by them.

Whenever I am inclined to feel this way, I tell myself, "We never lose. We learn." I used their criticism as research and get better at my craft.

What if we turn our scrolling and judgement into something productive? What if we become less reactive toward what we see and more curious instead? Let's talk about a common scenario, shall we? You see a picture of a celebrity online that's been manipulated to the point where they've lost their pores and resemble a doll more than a person.

Your first reaction might be to tell yourself how sad they are because of the over-editing. The image might make you uneasy. You jump to the comments and scroll through them, curious about what others are saying. Some are bold (or rude) enough to comment on it while others praise the person in the post.

You go through their feed next, trying to find an explanation for why they posted the photo. Whether you agree with the celebrity or not, their post got people are talking about them.

Remember the online challenge where people used cups to make their lips swollen because a celebrity popped up one day with new lips? The challenge was followed by the release of their lipstick line. No matter how you feel about them or their product, an audience was born.

Judgement turned into profit. Believe it or not, this can be a powerful marketing strategy. We follow stories due to controversy or inspiration. No one likes a boring character or narrative.

I am not one to say all press is good press. I believe every message has a messenger and a recipient, and we can take advantage of all the ways our story is interpreted.

Think about the last piece of content you saw that stirred something in you. Dissect why the video, photo, song, etc. provoked such a feeling. Were you laughing? Appalled? Did you tear up and send it to five friends you thought really needed to see it?

Google Madonna, and you'll find many articles talking about her artistry and message. I always found her to be a marketing genius. Every symbol, song, and her overall imagery was orchestrated to create followers and haters.

I don't want you to focus on whether you like or dislike her. Focus on how the loyalty of her fandom and critics gave her a platform that has remained for decades.

It's tough to forget what happened on August 28th, 2003 because of three pop icons: Britney, Christina, and Madonna. Were the performers belting out powerful notes? No. Were the dance moves impeccable? No. But God, just having those three women sharing a stage was an experience. If you are a millennial, you know where I'm going with this.

The image of Madonna coming out of that cake will forever live in my head. The smirk. The way she started singing "Hollywood." The entire performance revolved around her and, once again, had us acknowledging she is the queen of pop. And how could we forget the kiss? I remember going to work at Market Basket in Ashland, Massachusetts and seeing every magazine plastered with their faces.

Madonna defended and fought for the LGBTQIA+ community back when progress wasn't as evident. She used her art, music, body, and image to send a message.

It is in judgement that a real audience is born. The next time you are judging someone online, pay attention to why they made you feel something in the first place. Look beyond your own narrative. What makes millions of people follow them? Which of their actions has drawn praise and criticism?

IT IS IN JUDGEMENT
THAT AN AUDIENCE
IS BORN.

FRIENDS, CONNECTIONS, AND GROWTH PARTNERS

I want to make something clear. There's nothing wrong with wanting something from someone. You want your friend's company, your boss's money, your partner's love. You want the ending of the book to be good or the villain to die. The list goes on and on. Too often, we're taught that wanting something out of a situation is wrong. But going into a situation without clear direction is dangerous. It'd be like sailing without a compass or flying without instruments.

This can be the make or break for many. It's important to foster meaningful relationships to reach your goals, because your money is in the pockets of who you know. Regardless of your expertise, you need the support of others.

Let's talk about connections where friendship may or may not be part of the package. The first thing you must understand is there are friendships, connections, and growth partners.

FRIENDSHIPS

Friendships are part of your circle. Those you hang out with simply for the joy of their company. You are not after anything other than their presence. Sometimes, these can indeed lead to incredible networking opportunities.

I have been, and still am, fortunate to have those friends in my life—people who desire my company first and realize we can be bridges to each other second. Friendships that evolve into meaningful bridges are great. But in the art of fostering those relationships, one must always set boundaries. And if you flinched at that word, this is where you need to pay really close attention. Boundaries exist when you want to keep something or someone around. Otherwise, you simply walk away. Boundaries are good. They are healthy. And they matter.

I always make it clear that if an opportunity arises from a friend, we have the freedom to speak our minds without judgment. I am the friendship-first guy in these scenarios. Having healthy conversations will amount to many more years of companionship.

CONNECTIONS

These are the people you meet in business environments. Your first approach here isn't friendship. You aren't looking to invite them out for dinner or get to know them. You are, in fact, after something they can give you. Whether it be a phone number, a referral, a job, or a post to strengthen your brand online.

You don't meet these people at your aunt's house. They are at very particular events and environments. Sometimes clients ask me about this approach. They are embarrassed or think they are being intrusive when walking up to someone in one of these environments.

Let me share what I always tell them: Read the room. If you are at a networking event, then by all means, when you see a person grazing by the cheese station, go talk to them. That's why they are there. If you are, let's say, at a talk, look for a person who might be the bridge—their assistant, social media manager, etc. But this isn't a green flag for you to be abrasive or scream, "Look at me!"

We are in the business of feeling. Before walking up to someone, think about the ways you can contribute to their journey. What can you offer? This is where we turn to our life experience. Let's say you are a divorcee and the person you want to approach built a successful business after a divorce. Be honest about who you are and your desire to do the same. Always start the conversation with an emotional hook.

There are two possible scenarios when people walk up to me wanting to know how I got started in writing and creative entrepreneurship. The ones who get my attention are the ones who bring their stories to the table.

"J.D., I've been writing this book for five years. I've queried so many agents and nothing. I've tried self-publishing, but I can't, for the life of me, find my readership. What now?"

"J.D., I've always loved art. I've been dabbling with graphic design and fell in love with it, but my family can't put me through school. What do I do now?"

Start a conversation with a meaningful sentence and you've got my attention. Here are a few examples of conversations that went nowhere.

"Man, I see you hustling. How much did you have to make to buy [insert object of desire here]."

"I want to be rich. Got any tips?"

"My father is so and so, and I'd love a free design in exchange for a promo."

Connections will not always evolve into friendships. And that's okay. Your agent might never be your best friend. The CEO of some company might never come over for dinner. Your event planner might never go fishing with you. And that's okay.

The dynamics of these relationships are for mutual gains pertaining to finance, branding, and marketing. There's nothing wrong with fostering these relationships. It'd be wrong to not aim for them.

These are friends who are in the same, or similar, industry as you. They are the people you call when you achieve something major. They are your cheerleaders, not your competitors.

These might be the toughest to find out of the three. I've been in the industry for over a decade and though I know many people, few have become growth partners.

You don't need a large group. One will do. Whenever I have a new release, my friends and family congratulate me, and life goes on. That's fine, but when I share my accomplishments with my growth partners, we celebrate with tears and drinks and food.

These are the people who stay in your life through the hurdles of your industry. They become mentors, people you call for advice only they can give.

It took me nearly ten years to find an agent and get a "traditional" book deal. I questioned my skills, worth, and heritage. Am I not Brazilian enough? American enough? Talented enough? Is all I've built not enough?

My growth partners encouraged me. They kept me accountable during my search and my sanity in check. They reminded me time and time again that it wasn't about my talent, but about someone else's ability to connect with what I was doing.

THERE'S NOTHING
WRONG WITH WANTING
SOMETHING FROM
SOMEONE.

THE BIG ILLUSION

To build a strong brand, narrative, and connection with your audience, you must let go of the illusion that every space is for you. This comes from a place of experience. I think at this point of our conversation, you've noticed that for many years, I wanted to belong to modern Christianity. I clipped my wings and tamed my thoughts so I could be part of that crowd. While I learned skills I could apply to my career (hello, public speaking), I also diminished a lot of who I was so I could be who they wanted me to be.

The fact of the matter was simple. Regardless of my talent or accomplishments, I was gay. I would never belong to that club, no matter how much I wanted to fool myself into thinking I did.

I started working as a graphic designer and author during a time when I longed for acceptance. I've mentioned this before, but while writing my first book, I held back a lot of the ideas I had for the story because I was a church boy. In my head, I wanted something with more meat (literally). I toned myself down for those around me.

I was a teenager dealing with my undocumented status and grappling with my professional journey. To make myself smaller and more ordinary, I built a narrative that I was the good Christian boy venturing into entrepreneurship. I was "God's messenger" to the secular.

Those around me ate the message up. I felt like some glorified Christian spy going out into the world to plant a seed. Some part of me wanted to fully embrace this so-called mission. I was proud of what I accomplished in my early twenties, but I knew I was betraying myself. That narrative resonated with me because I wanted to belong, even though I wasn't designed to. While some of the preached values were good, their core belief resented me for who I was.

There are moments where you either take a stand or settle for being in a complacent state forever. One Sunday morning in July, we played a gorgeous set. I remember the congregation engaging deeply. When we finished, the speaker started exposing private affairs shared to them by members of the church out of spite. They proceeded to take shots at me and the musicians because we hadn't fully "obeyed" the God-command for a fast that year.

My blood boiled. I looked at the camera streaming the service online, walked up on stage, grabbed my gear, and left. I recall thinking that with my every step, I was taking a public stand for myself.

In environments like that, curiosity is confused with rebellion. That's what they labelled me as after I walked off stage. A rebel. When I met with the leadership, I was told to disregard the way the pastor spoke that day. To simply focus on how much that pastor loved me. The leadership encouraged me to believe love should matter more their actions.

It was during that uncomfortable conversation that I embraced the truth I knew all along. I must be respected in every space, but I will never belong in all of them. A weight was lifted from my shoulders.

After enduring years of verbal and mental abuse, I decided to find my crowd—friends and entrepreneurs alike. The farther I walked from the place I was never meant to belong, the more I expanded and thrived. Yes, it was frightening to step outside of the only universe I'd ever known, but it was worth every moment.

We find excuses to stay in those types of places because it's comfortable. Certain environments clip the wings of creative entrepreneurs because we are told "no," instead of "take a chance." It's a dangerous thing to settle.

A lot is said about respect and acceptance. I believe in respect. You must be respected everywhere. Your journey, identity, background—all the things that make you unique deserve it. Now, acceptance? Your conservative parents might never accept your sexuality. Dad thought you were going to take over the business, but you decided to move to a different country. That preacher might never accept gay marriage. But you have to stand up for yourself and find your community. Whether those people accept you is on them, but they must respect you. Or you must remove yourself from their space.

Respect is honoring someone's courage to be authentic. Audiences follow mission and heart, so if you aren't rooted in this truth, you will be building castles in the sand.

I wish I'd been bolder and more honest with myself and my audience, but I can't go back. I can only use those experiences moving forward. If you are in an environment that holds back your creativity, then take a breath. This isn't a demand to up and leave immediately. This is hopefully a spark. May it turn it into a flame when you are ready.

TO BUILD A STRONG BRAND, NARRATIVE, AND CONNECTION WITH YOUR AUDIENCE, YOU MUST LET GO OF THE ILLUSION THAT EVERY SPACE IS FOR YOU.

STAY CURIOUS

No matter how good something is, it'll only remain that way if the experience is a pleasant one. While I'd love to extend our chat, I believe making it short and sweet is what will make it memorable. And the coffee shop we're in is taking last call.

I have thought long and hard about these last few moments. What can I say to leave my coffee companion inspired to head out into the unknown with boldness and courage?

Stay curious. I know, I know. You've heard it a million times. You might even call the saying cliché. But I've come to realize that what we call cliché is often a truth we should carry with us. We get used to the things that matter, and what should always be extraordinary ends up becoming the opposite. In this case, it's overused because it helps.

Staying curious matters now more than ever. Algorithms rule what we see and how we interact. Our every move is tracked. These platforms are wiring our brains to believe we must be fed information instead of being curious.

When you think about it, algorithms tend to distract us from the choices we make. We follow creators, but never see their posts. Instead, we scroll and scroll through content suggested to us. The danger of constant suggestion is the abdication of intent. When we have too much to choose from, we take longer to make a decision. Go to a restaurant with a million items on the menu, and you'll see for yourself.

Our brains are being told to drift instead of sail. Every suggestion becomes an idea. Every idea becomes a task. And just like that, we are overwhelmed with to-dos, with no mental space for our curiosity. In truth, we shouldn't be drifting, we should be the ones steering the course, using the wind and stars to find our way.

This does not mean we should diminish our curiosity for the sake of the path we're on. Curiosity opens the doors to possibility and keeps you intentional about your goals and decisions. Everything we see and touch was a curious thought in someone's mind at some point. The reason we advanced as a society is because the curious decided to do something intentional with those ideas.

Think about it. You have this wonderful idea and want to develop it into something tangible. So you have to stick it out. You do what needs to be done to get to the end. Branding, narrative, and audience building require a constant flow of curious ideas. Without curiosity, inspiration will fade, and apathy will creep in, halting progress.

I never settled for the surface. When I bought a Tamagotchi, I took care of it for a few weeks before unscrewing it to see how it worked. I knew underneath the pink plastic case was an extremely complicated system that gave life to the little beast.

Bible school on Sundays? I was the one asking the teacher all sorts of questions about the dos and don'ts they taught.

To stay curious as a creative entrepreneur is to revisit the spirit we had when we were first discovering the world. That sense of adventure (which we often abandon as we age) can be a powerful tool to invent and reinvent yourself.

It's curiosity that inspires you to research and create. You chose to stick around for the end of this conversation because of curiosity. You could've given up halfway and said, "Nah, this isn't my cup of tea (or coffee)." Yet here you are.

No progress was made without a curious mind. Get to the end of what you are working on. See your project completed. Do it for you, for those who came before you, and for all those who will come after. And remember, you are not for everybody.

TO STAY CURIOUS AS A
CREATIVE ENTREPRENEUR
IS TO REVISIT THE SPIRIT WE
HAD WHEN WE WERE FIRST
DISCOVERING THE WORLD.

OTHER TITLES BY J.D. NETTO

The Broken Miracle Duology

The Broken Miracle: Part One

The Broken Miracle: Part Two

Henderbell

Henderbell: The Shadow of Saint Nicholas

Henderbell: The Shadow of Saint Nicholas (Special Christmas Edition)

Henderbell: Whispers in the Dark

Anthologies

Saved by the Page: Forty-Five Stories Written

by Readers Saved by Books (Edited by J.D. Netto)

The Echoes of Fallen Stars

The Echoes of Fallen Stars: Immortal Crowns

The Echoes of Fallen Stars: Gods and Mortals

The Other Side of the Ocean

June 2025

9 798218 484125